The Face Tattoo Mugshots

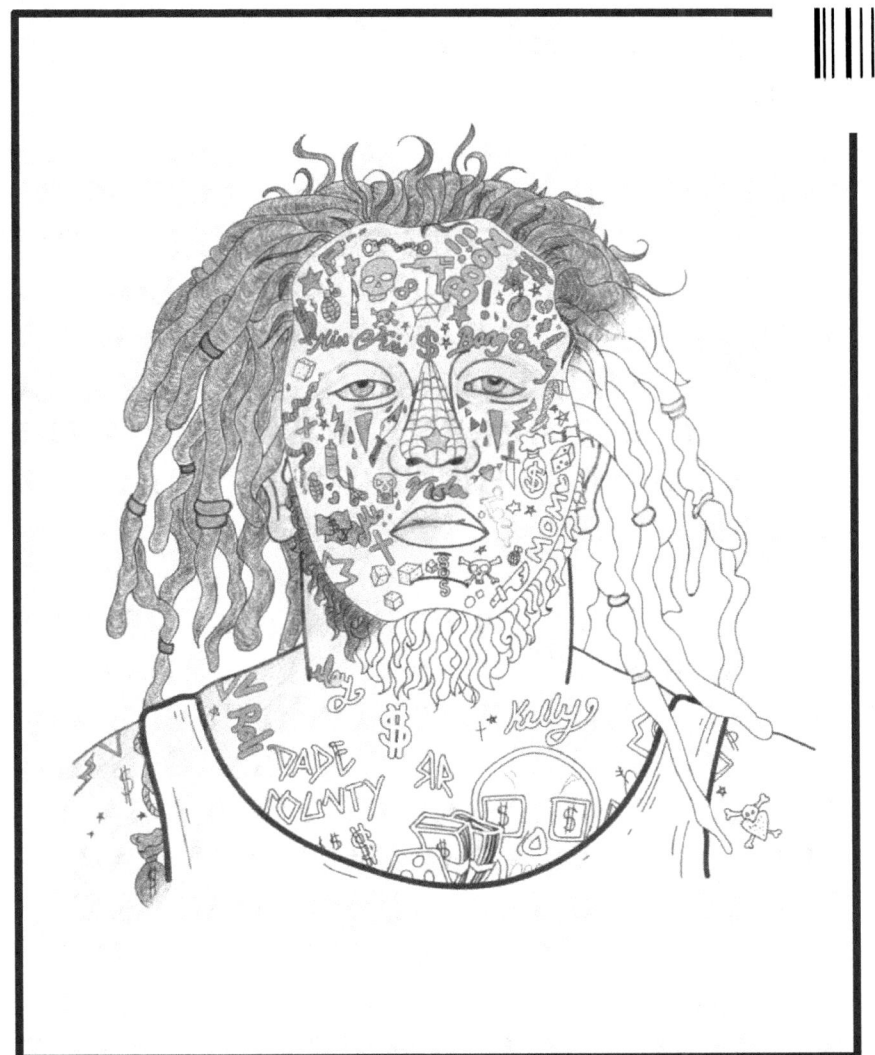

Adult Coloring Book

By Giovanni Verbania
Edited by Jennifer Anne Gomez

Verbania
P.O. BOX 2663 Sausalito CA 94965
Copyright 2017
All Rights Reserved

ISBN-13: 978-1982085124
ISBN-10: 1982085126

Disclaimer

Contents

The History of Face Tattoos

Human beings started tattooing themselves as soon as they could fashion needles, stick ink on them, and jab them in their skin. Ötzi, a Tyrolean Alps iceman, was buried and mummified beneath a glacier around 3250 B.C. He had 61 tattoos all over his body. In 2016, researchers discovered a 3000 year old Egyptian mummy with over 30 tattoos covering her head to toe. Victorian aristocrats even enjoyed a brief fad with tattoos, inked elites including **Czar Nicholas II, Kaiser Wilhelm, and King George V.**

Face tattoos hold a special place in human culture. The Māori of New Zealand used elaborate and beautiful face markings called *Tā moko* to advertise high social status. But in ancient Rome, facial tattoos were reserved for escaped slaves and criminals to mark them for life. Women in the tribes of Mali tattoo their lips before and after marriage as symbols of beauty and belonging. Similarly, indigenous people of Japan, Taiwan, and Myanmar also tattooed their faces to denote tribal membership or marriage status. In Western society, face tattoos typically belong to two groups of enthusiasts: "modern primitives" obsessed with piercings and body modification, or prison inmates and gang members. It is the ink enthusiasts in the latter category depicted in this book.

In United States prisons, tattooing is illegal, so inmates have to carefully improvise tattooing equipment from guitar strings, mechanical pencils, radio transistors or paperclips. Ink is made from soot or burnt and melted chess pieces, Bible pages, toothpaste, or ballpoint pen caps. Despite these difficulties, face tattoos are gaining in popularity with penitentiary guests and prison tattoo artists are among the most widely respected and wealthy prisoners.

Today, 36 percent of Americans aged 18-25 have at least one tattoo. In 2003 American boxer Mike Tyson got a large tribal tattoo on his face. In 2012 Canadian DJ Deadmau5 got a star tattooed under his right eye. Pop music teen sensation Justin Bieber had a tiny cross tattooed under his right eye in 2016. As our cultural tastes and attitudes evolve, so will social acceptance of the face tattoo. Isn't it time you rethought your resistance to the stunning and beautiful art of face tattoos? Face it- you want one!

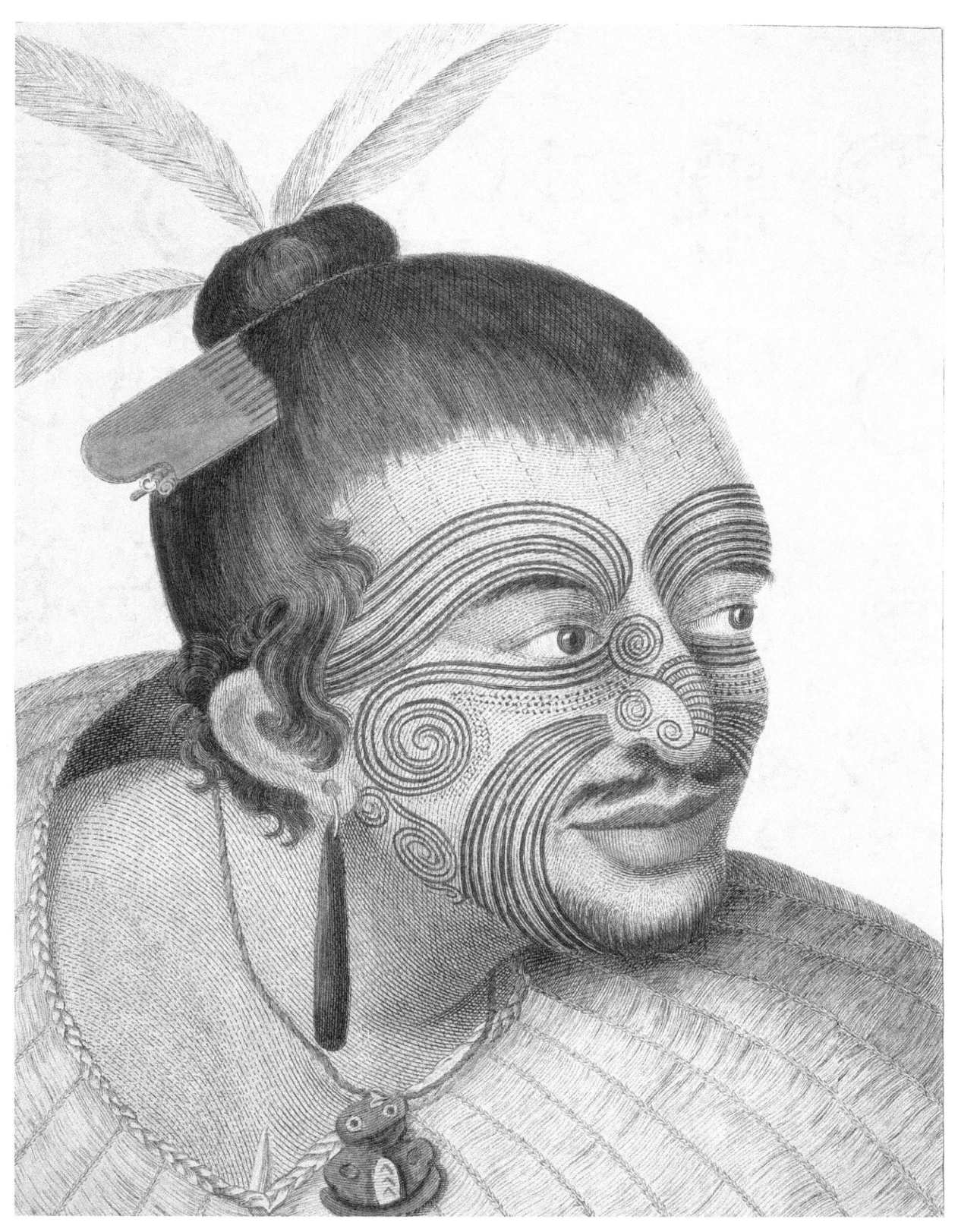

Maori Chief
Sydney Parkinson, 1784.

Color Test Page

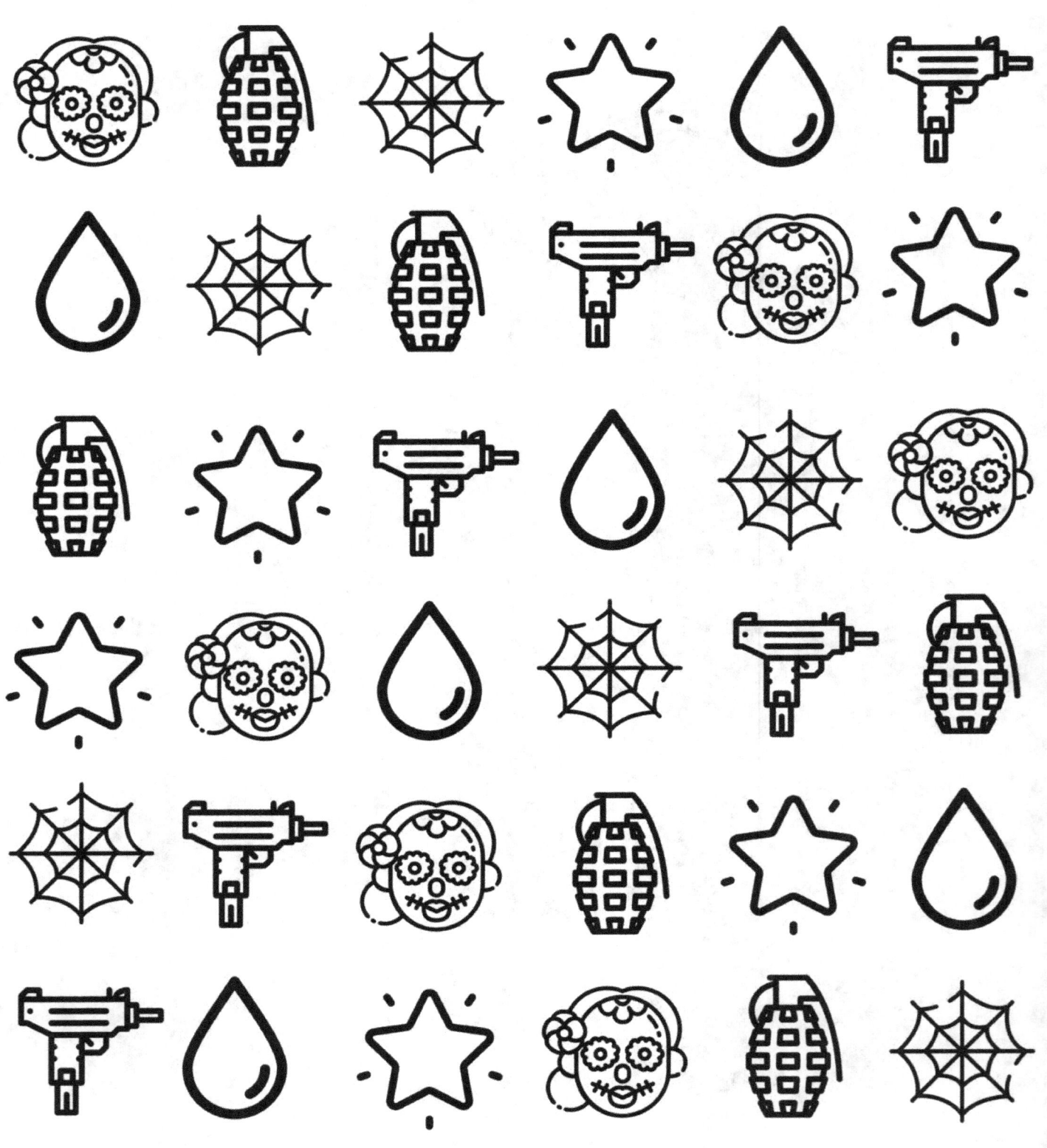

Author's Note

Face tattoos...I remember clearly the first time I saw someone with a face tattoo in person. He was a 19 or 20 year old fellow student in a drawing class I had at community college. In the middle of his forehead was a small swastika similar to Charles Manson's. Curiosity overwhelmed me- why would he do that? Was he a skinhead? An Aryan? A psycho? He turned out to be a Native American. Maybe it was an ancient native symbol?

 I asked him as carefully and courteously as possible about his tattoo, which probably came out something like, "So what's up with the swastika dude?" I wasn't sure if I was about to get my ass kicked or make a new friend honestly, but I had to know. He was super friendly about it, but looked down and into the distance and just said, "Well, I made some mistakes when I was younger, but that's the past." I didn't ask him about the past and we never spoke about it again. He proved to be an amazing artist. I always wondered what had possessed him to get the tattoo- had he been in prison?

Years later I was having my carpets cleaned in San Francisco and the crew lead was a hulking Latino guy covered in tattoos, including a small blue teardrop near his eye. I'd grown up around Cholos who had a few tattoos, but not like this guy. Was he in one of San Francisco's many gangs? Was he an Ex-con? I'd heard all sorts of meanings ascribed to tear tattoos: one for each year in jail, one for each murder committed, one for fellow gang-members that were killed. What was his for?

I never got the nerve to ask him about it, but I remember thinking that cleaning carpets was probably the only legit job this guy was going to get from now on. At least he was going straight. Then he offered to clean the sofas and drapes "off the clock" for a deeply discounted cash rate. Part of me was disappointed he was double-crossing his employer who had so generously given him a job despite the face tattoo. Part of me admired his ingenuity and hustle: he was going to need any and all income sources to survive. I took the offer. Had I paid a killer- or just someone that had "made some mistakes when they were younger?"

GIOVANNI VERBANIA 2017

Jorge Mario Aguirre

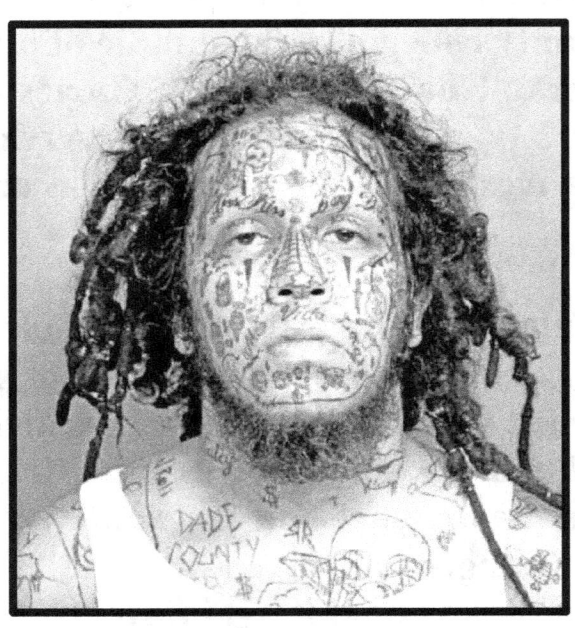

DISTINGUISHING TATS: SPIDER WEB ON NOSE, "MI VIDA LOCA" ON TOP LIP, "KISS KISS BANG BANG" ON EYEBROWS, UZI MACHINE GUN ON FOREHEAD, CLOWN TEARS ABOVE AND BELOW EYES.

DOB: 8/27/1986
ARREST DATES: 4/25/2010, 8/21/2010
CHARGES: BATTERY, CHILD ABUSE/NO HARM, ASSAULT/AGG/FIREARM, CONTROLLED SUBSTANCE POSSESSION
RANGE: MIAMI-DADE COUNTY, FLORIDA
GANG AFFILIATION: UNKNOWN

NOTES: PULLED OVER FOR OVERLY TINTED WINDOWS, JORGE ACTUALLY HAS THE MIAMI-DADE AREA CODE "305" TATTOOED ON HIS CHIN, NOT "SOS." "MI VIDA LOCA" IS SPANISH FOR "MY CRAZY LIFE."

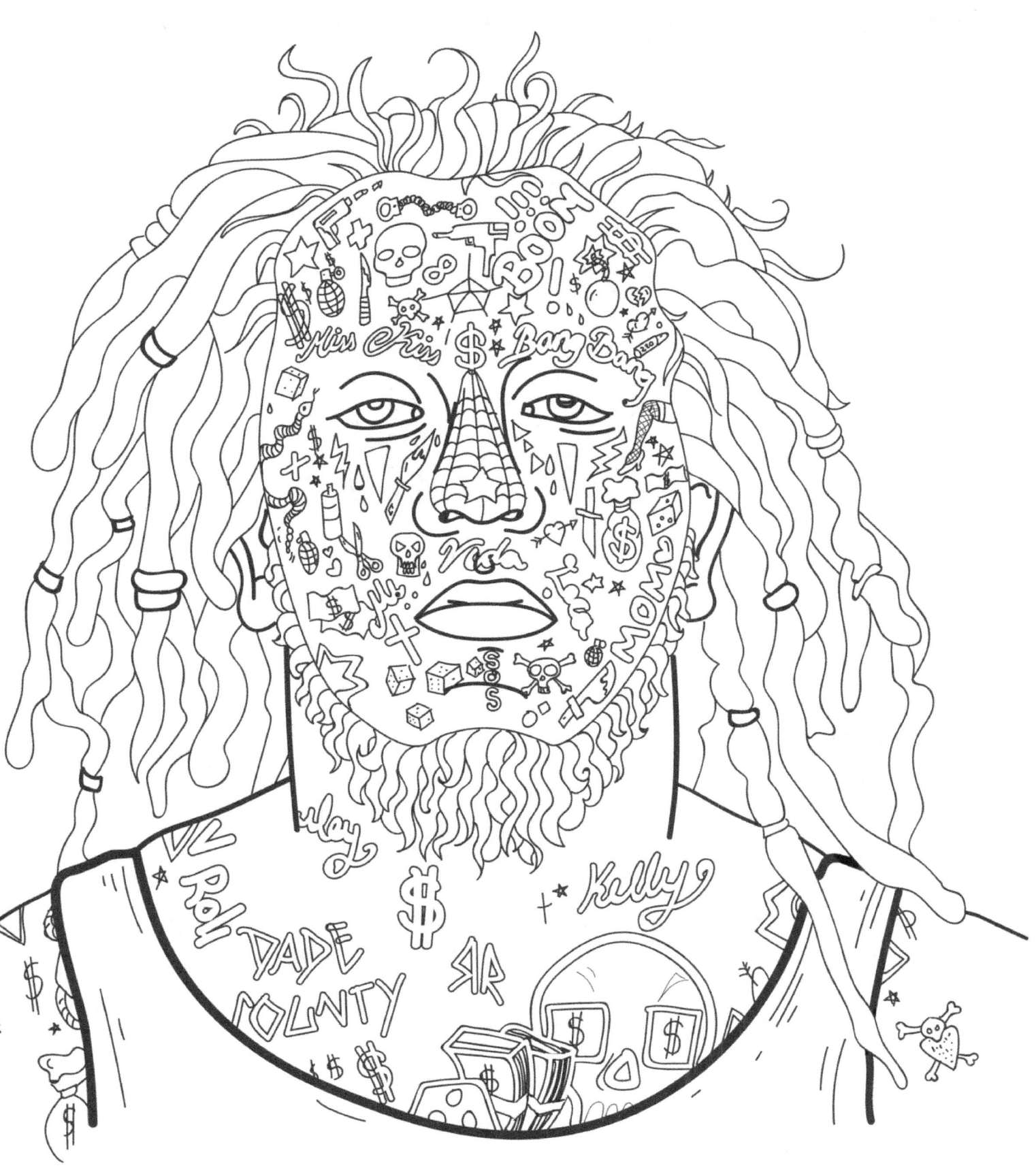

Kenneth Dewain Parker

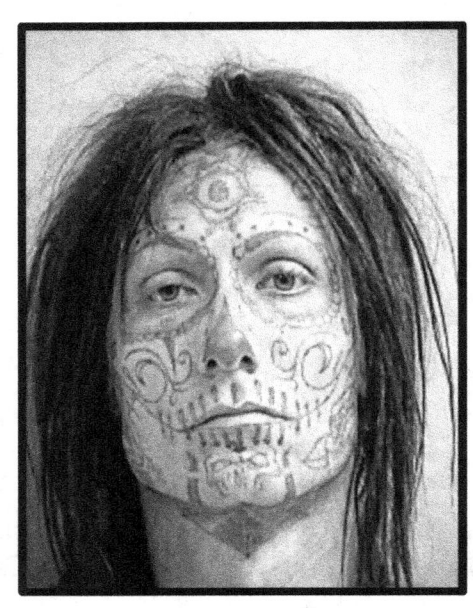

DISTINGUISHING TATS: THIRD EYE ON FOREHEAD, STITCHED MOUTH, SUGAR SKULL-STYLE EYES

DOB: 11/19/1983
ARREST DATES: HALLOWEEN NIGHT 2014
CHARGES: (SECOND DEGREE MISDEMEANOR) LOITERING OR PROWLING
RANGE: FORT WALTON BEACH, FLORIDA
GANG AFFILIATION: UNKNOWN

NOTES: THE STITCHED MOUTH TATTOO MAY HAVE A DOUBLE MEANING: "LA CATARINA" - A DÍA DE LOS MUERTOS FIGURE THAT LAUGHS AT HUMAN FOLLY, AND "OMERTA" - THE MAFIA CODE OF SILENCE.

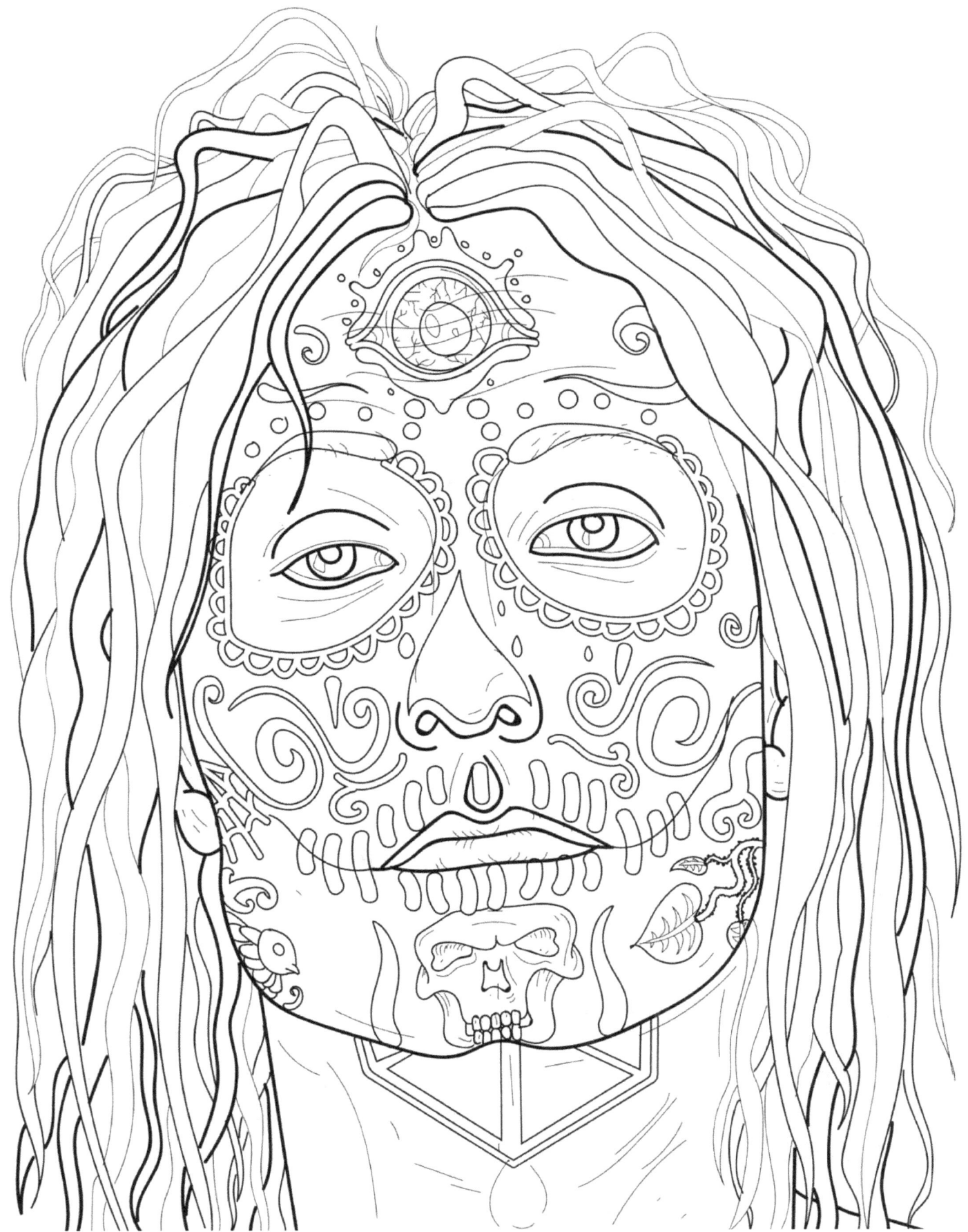

Robert Hardister

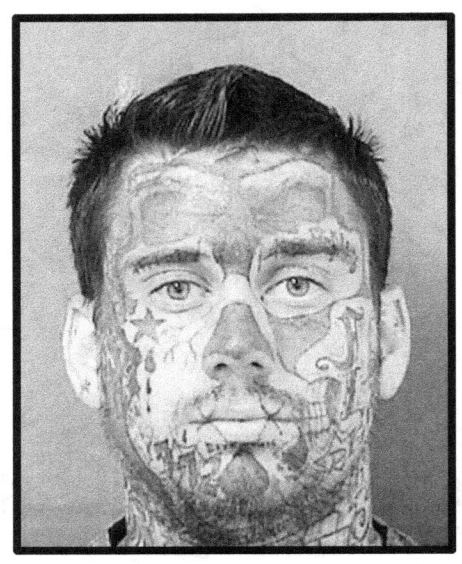

DISTINGUISHING TATS: "772" ON CHIN, "FL" ON LEFT CHEEK, ACE OF SPADES ON CHIN, SKELETON TEETH LEFT CHEEK, MOUTH STITCHES, EYEBROW STITCHES

DOB: 9/17/1991
ARREST DATES: ?/10/2009, ?/11/09/2010, ?/11/2011, ?/?/2012, 2/17/2013, 7/15/2016
CHARGES: STOLEN PROP-DEAL IN, FRAUD, GRAND THEFT MOTOR VEHICLE, PASS FORGED - ALTERED INSTRUMENT, FAILURE TO APPEAR, BURGL - UNOCCUPIED CONVEYANCE UNARMED, LARC - PETIT THEFT
RANGE: EAST COAST OF FLORIDA FROM PALM BEACH COUNTY TO ST. AUGUSTINE
GANG AFFILIATION: UNKNOWN

NOTES: 772 IS THE AREA CODE FOR MARTIN AND ST. LUCIE COUNTY ON THE EAST COAST OF SOUTH FLORIDA.

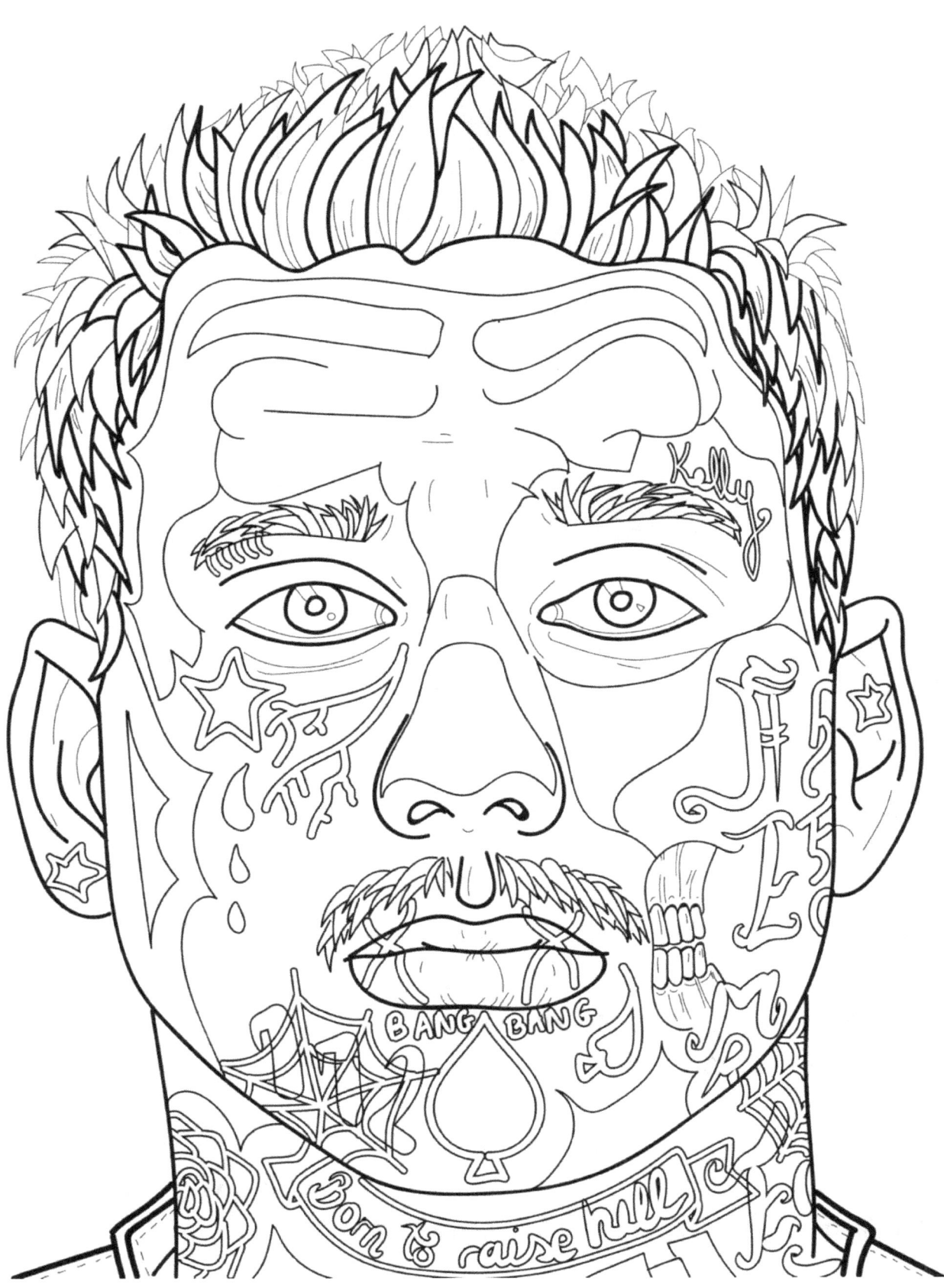

Phillip Katsabanis

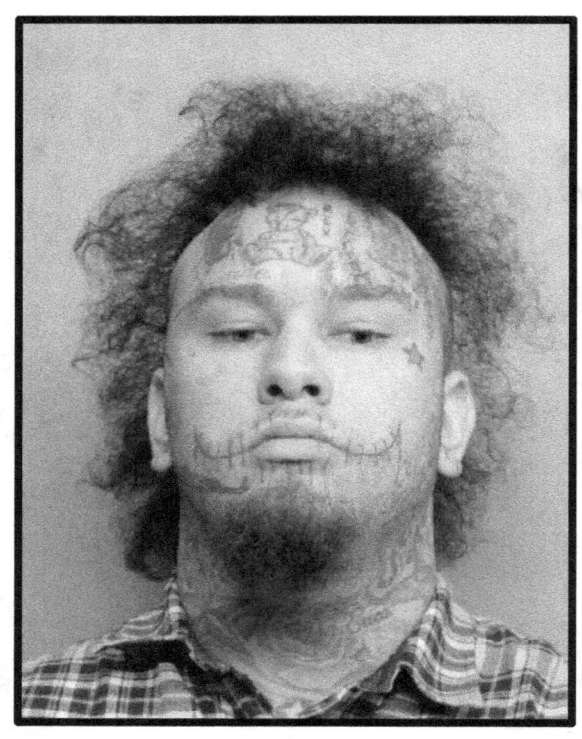

DISTINGUISHING TATS: STITCHED UP TEDDY BEAR ON FOREHEAD, STITCHED MOUTH, STITCHED SCARS ON FOREHEAD, "COCAINE" OVER RIGHT BROW, FRANKENSTEIN HEAD ON LEFT TEMPLE, AK-47 ON RIGHT CHEEK

DOB: 6/17/1995
ARREST DATES: 1/25/2017
CHARGES: FELONY GUN AND DRUG POSSESSION
RANGE: MIAMI FLORIDA AREA
GANG AFFILIATION: UNKNOWN

NOTES: PHILLIP KATSABANIS, AKA "STITCHES," WAS A CUBAN-GREEK RAPPER THAT ROSE TO FAME WITH INSTAGRAM AND YOUTUBE VIDEOS.

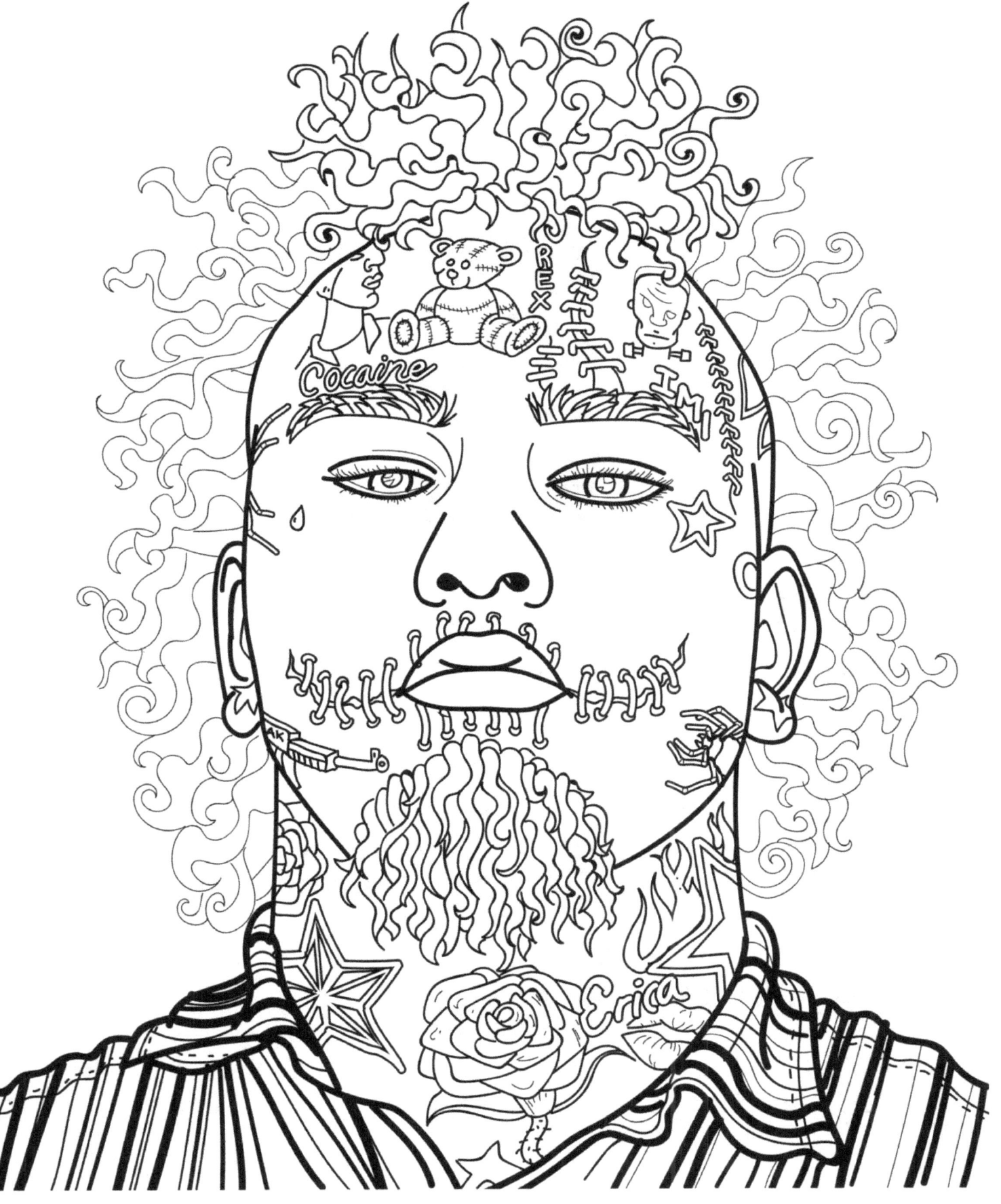

Jesse Russell AKA "Zombie"

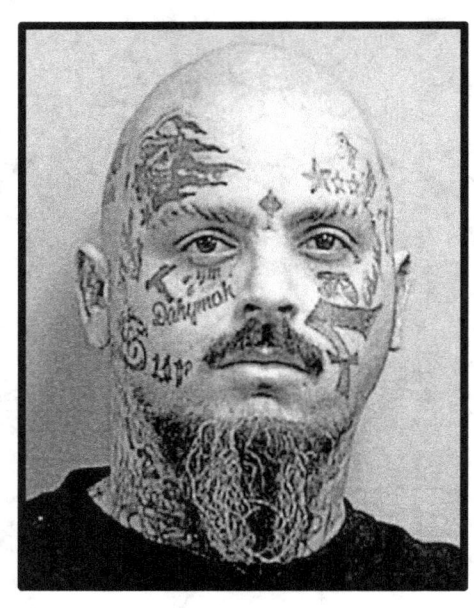

DISTINGUISHING TATS: UZI UNDER RIGHT EYE, SKULL PEEKING OUT OF RIGHT TEMPLE FISSURE, LARGE LETTER "F" OR BACKWARDS "7" ON LEFT CHEEK

DOB: 2/16/1981
ARREST DATES: 8/04/2011, 12/19/2011, 12/13/2012
CHARGES: ROBBERY - WITH FIREARM, PROB VIOLATION, DRUGS-POSSESSMARIJUANA-POSSESS - WIT SELL ETC WI 1000FT WORSHP/BUSN SCH III IV
RANGE: BOCA RATON TO PALM BEACH FLORIDA, FAILURE TO APPEAR
GANG AFFILIATION: UNKNOWN

NOTES: 7 MAY REFER TO "LUCKY 7," BUT F MAY MORE LIKELY REFER TO "FLORIDA"

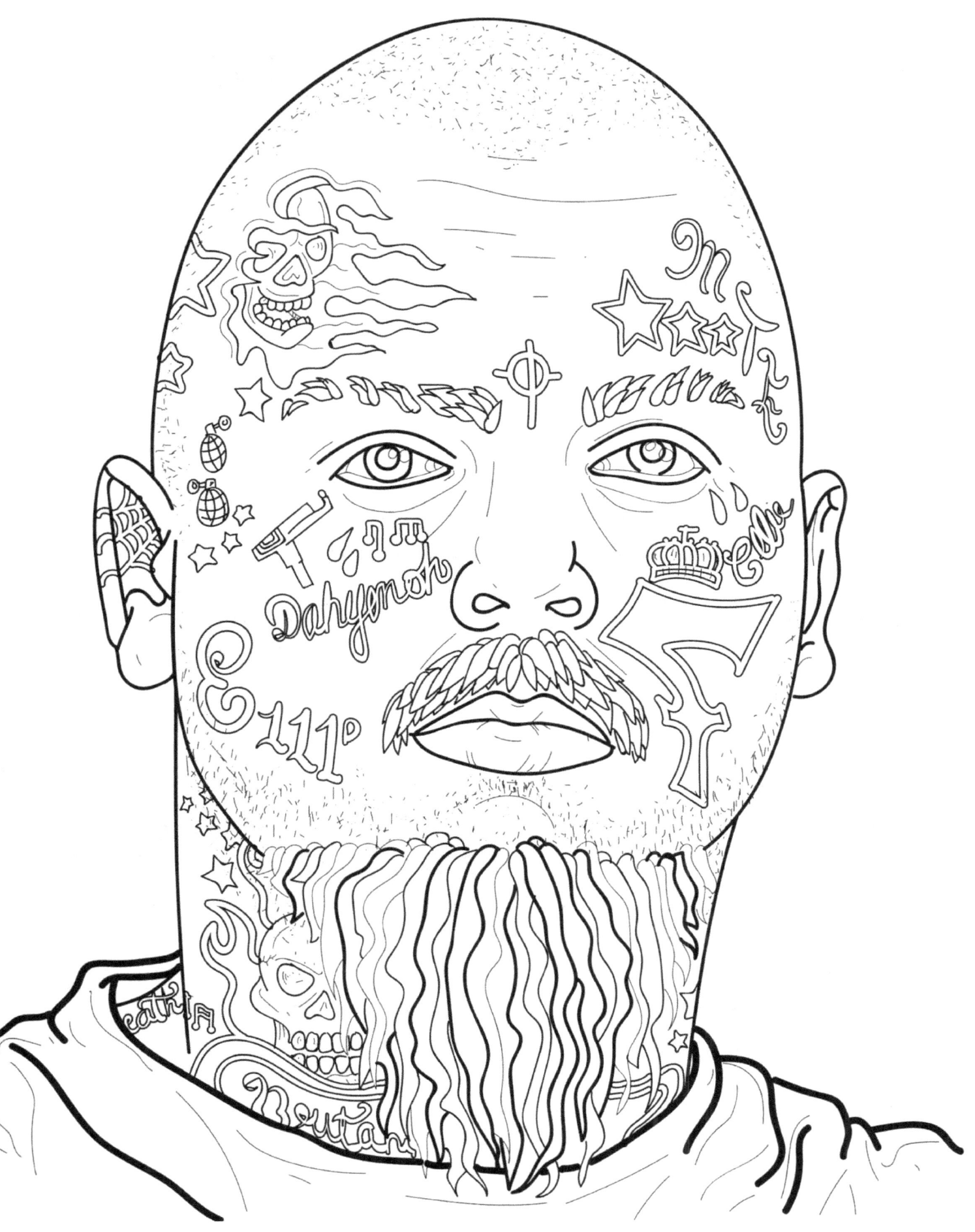

Khamprasong Thammavong

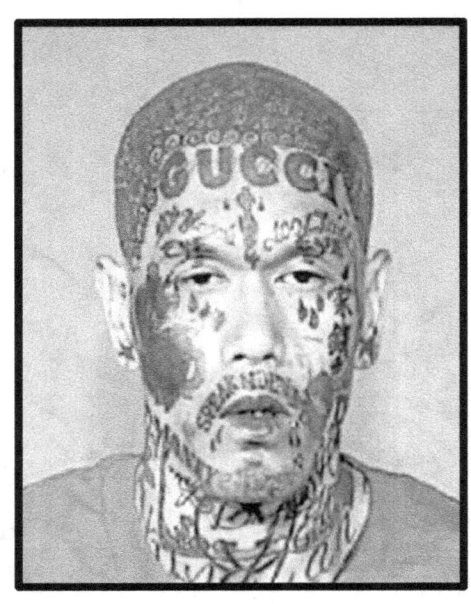

DISTINGUISHING TATS: "GUCCI" ON FOREHEAD, "SPEAK NO EVIL" ON UPPER LIP, "EYE" OVER EACH EYE, "100% BLOOD, 100% LOVE" ON EYEBROWS

DOB: 1982
ARREST DATES: 11/29/2012, 8/22/2013
CHARGES: VIOLATION OF PROBATION, POSSESS CONTROL SUBSTANCE, PERSON PORHIBITED FROM POSS A FIREARM SHALL NOT POSS AMMUNITION, LOADED FIREARM IN PUBLIC (PERSON OR VEHICLE)
RANGE: FRESNO COUNTY
GANG AFFILIATION: ALLEGED MEMBER OF LAOS BLOODS

NOTES: DID YOU KNOW? FRESNO HAS THE HIGHEST GANG POPULATION PER CAPITA AT 2.5% OF POPULATION OR 24,482 GANG BANGERS

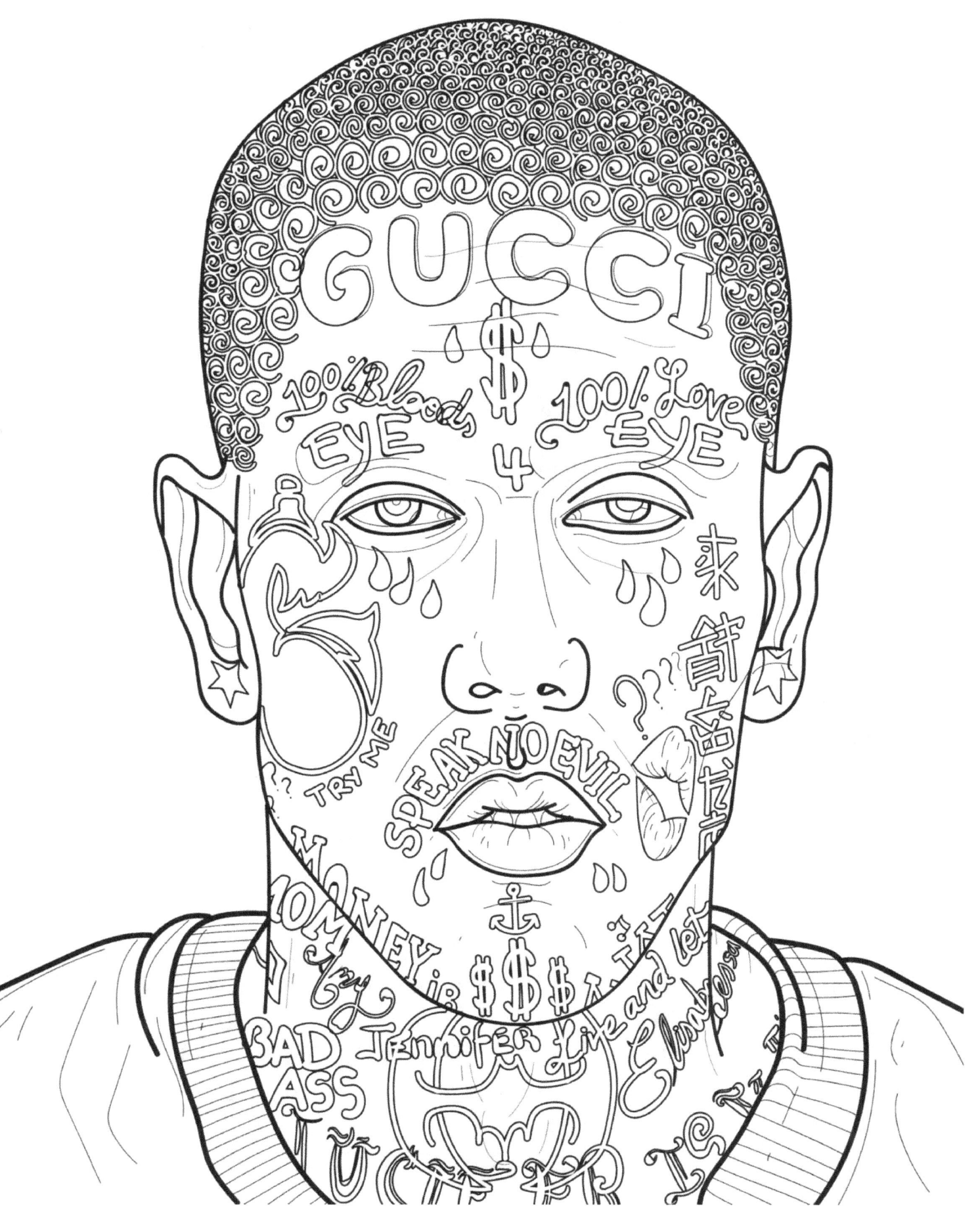

Keith Diaferia

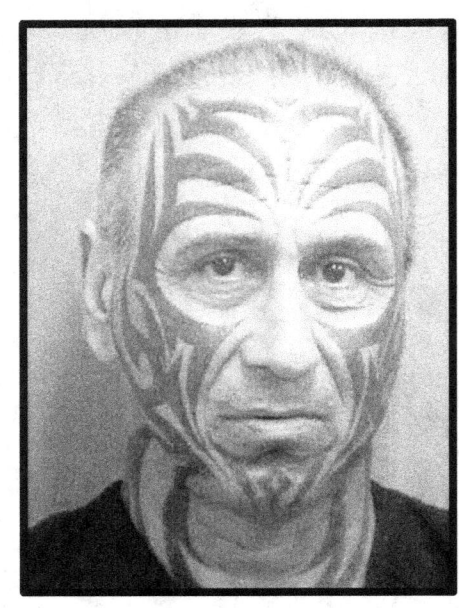

DISTINGUISHING TATS: UNUSUAL FOR A PRISONER, KEITH ONLY HAS FULL FACIAL TRIBAL TATTOOS

DOB: 2/26/1959
ARREST DATES: 7/29/2013,
CHARGES: DRUG EQUIP-POSSESS - AND OR USE, EVIDENCE-DESTROYING - TAMPER WITH OR FABRICATE PHYSICAL, POSS NARCOTIC CONTROLSUB
RANGE: PALM BEACH COUNTY FLORIDA
GANG AFFILIATION: UNKNOWN

NOTES: CAUGHT SMOKING CRACK IN HIS CAR. POLICE ALSO FOUND TWO NEEDLES CONTAINING HEROIN, FIVE EMPTY NEEDLES, THREE SMALL BAGGIES CONTAINING HEROIN, ONE CLEAR BAGGIE WITH RESIDUE INSIDE, ONE CRACK COCAINE ROCK, TWO EMPTY GREEN BAGGIES, ONE BLUE CRACK PIPE, ONE CLEAR CRACK PIPE, AND SOME PILLS.

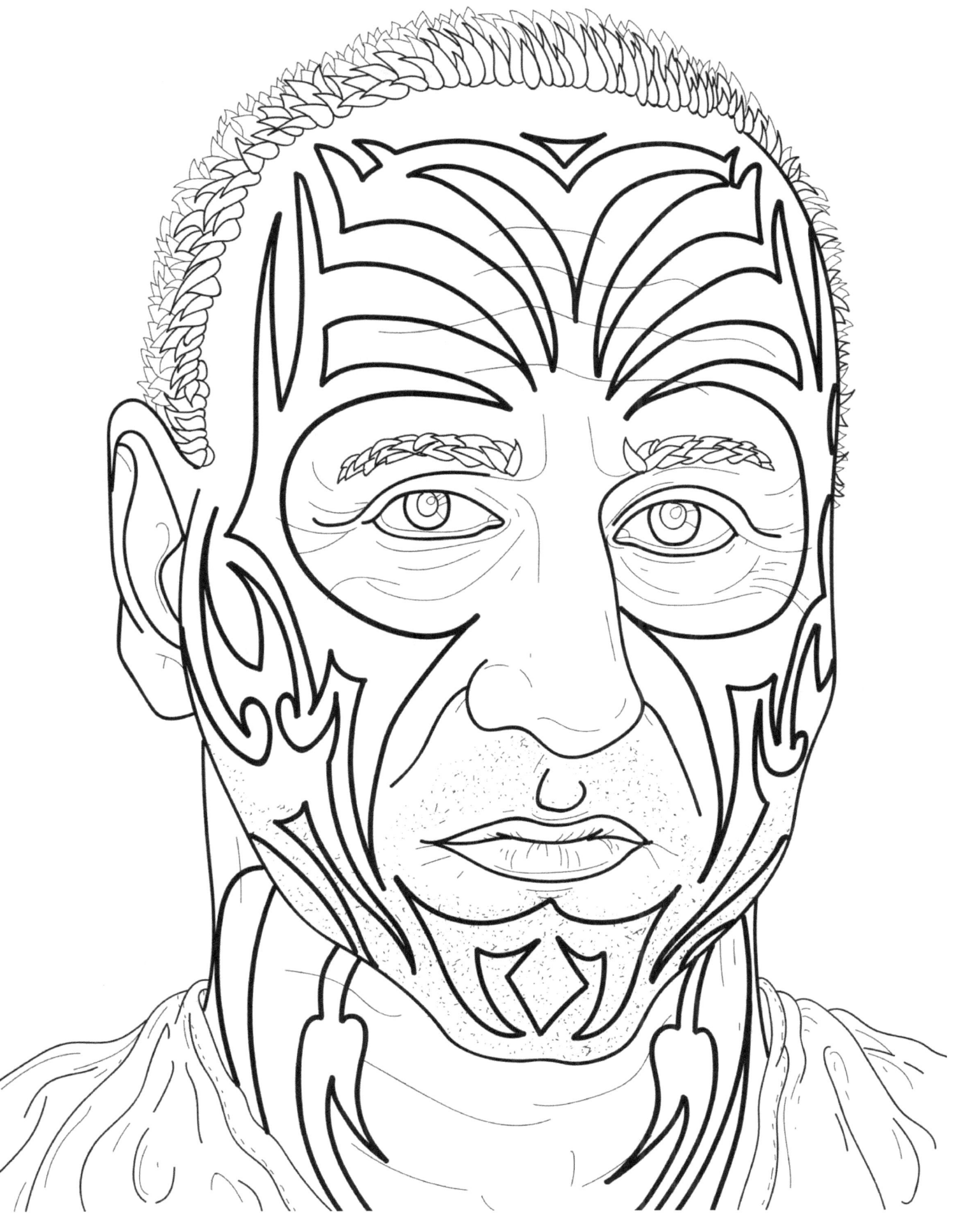

Michigan Man

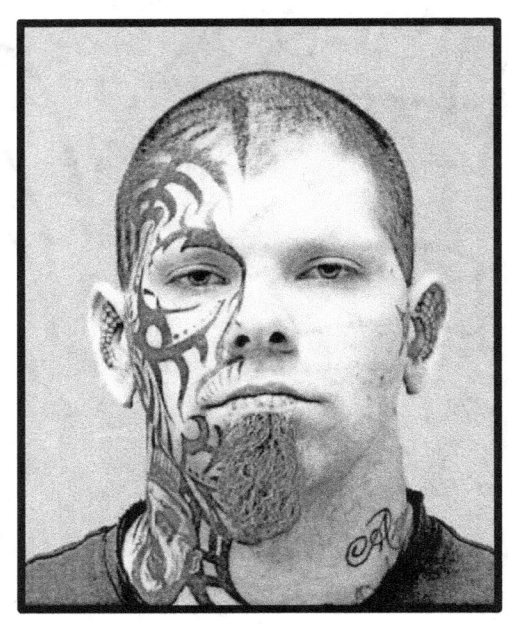

DISTINGUISHING TATS: TRIBAL TATTOO OVER ENTIRE RIGHT HEAD, SCREAMING UNCLE SAM HEAD ON NECK, SPDER WEB EARS.

DOB: UNKNOWN
ARREST DATES: UNKNOWN
CHARGES: UNKNOWN
RANGE: MICHIGAN
GANG AFFILIATION: UNKNOWN

NOTES: MICHIGAN MAN'S WHEREABOUTS, CHARGES, HISTORY AND TRUE NAME HAVE PROOVEN HARD TO TRACK DOWN

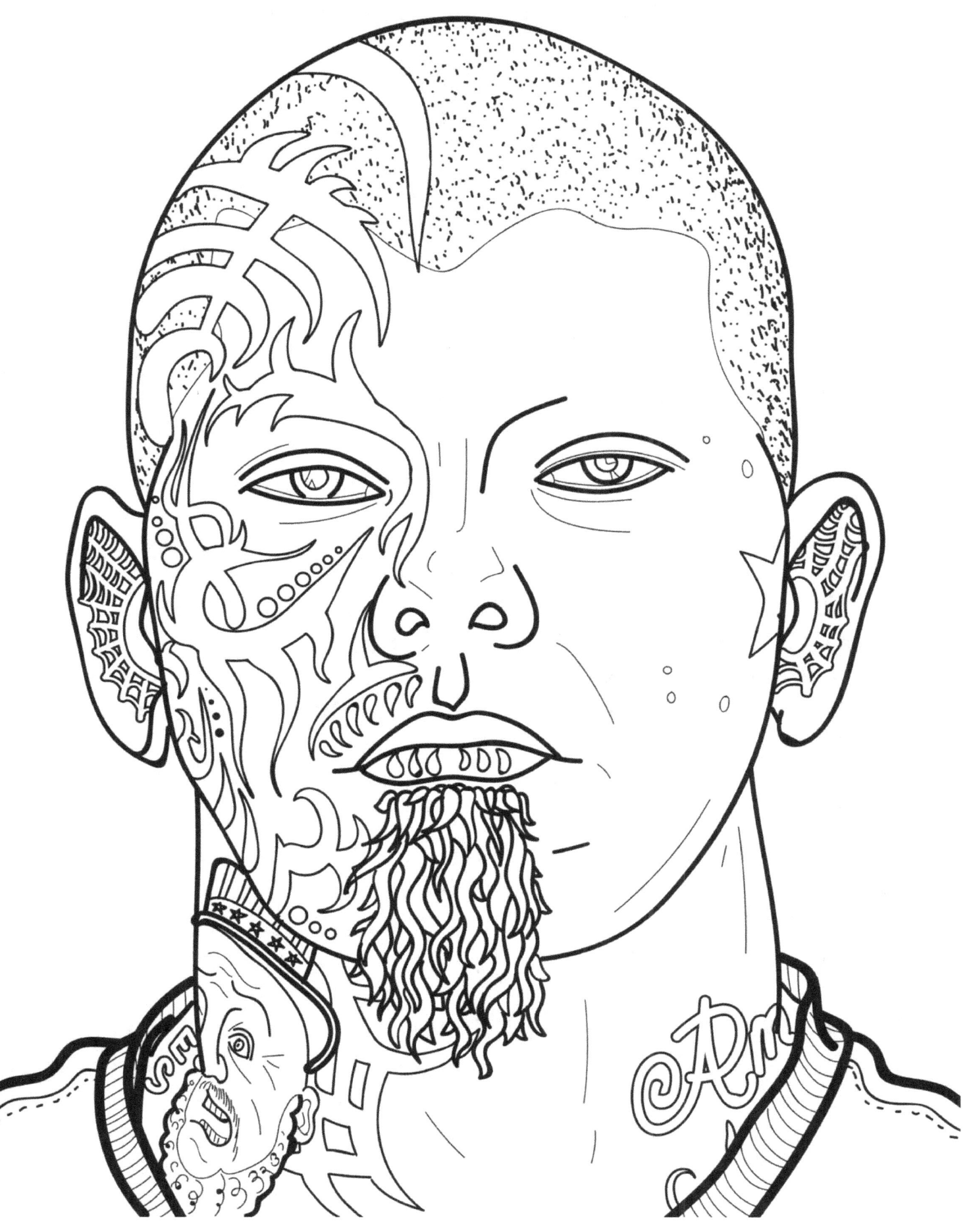

James Riani

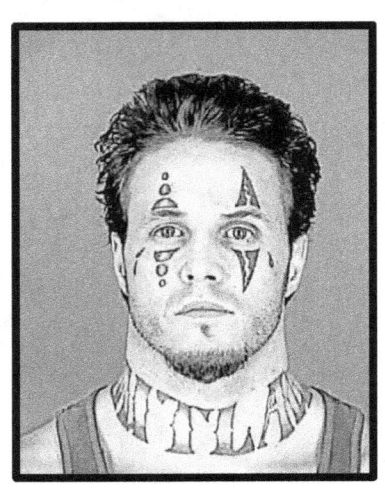

DISTINGUISHING TATS: STYLIZED CLOWN-STYLE MAKEUP MARKS ABOVE AND BELOW BOTH EYES, "OUTLAW" AROUND NECK

DOB: 3/7/1980
ARREST DATES: 12/03/2000, 1/27/2001, 2/12/2001, 2/18/2001, 7/21/2008, 1/07/2010, 10/07/2010, 8/08/2011
CHARGES: BURGLARY-STRUCTURE, POSSESS/INTRO CNTRBND-JAIL, POSSESSION DRUG PARAPHERNALIA, POSSESSION OF BURGLARY TOOLS, VIOL PROBATION MISDEMEANOR, POSSESS AND OR SALE OF CONTROLLED SUB, POSSES OF FIREARM BY FELON, POSS OF COCAINE, GRAND THEFT, DUI
RANGE: HERNANDO TO TAMPA COUNTIES FLORIDA
GANG AFFILIATION: ALLEGED MEMBER OF GANGSTER DISCIPLE STREET GANG ACCORDING TO U.S. ATTORNEY'S OFFICE

NOTES: SENTENCED TO 24 YEARS AND SEVEN MONTHS IN FEDERAL PRISON FOR POSSESSION WITH INTENT TO DISTRIBUTE METHAMPHETAMINE, POSSESSION OF FIREARM DURING DRUG TRAFFICKING

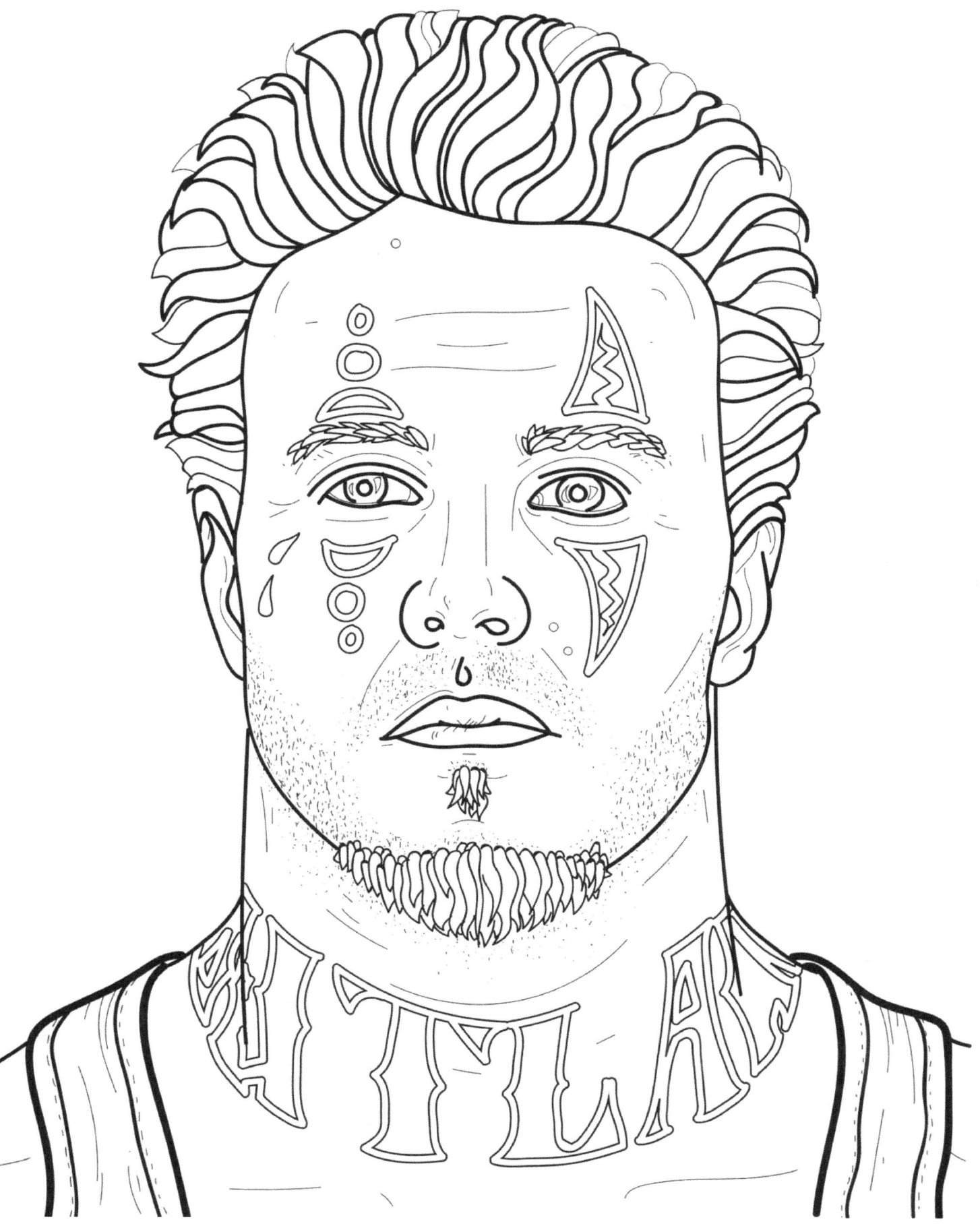

Rayzale Scott

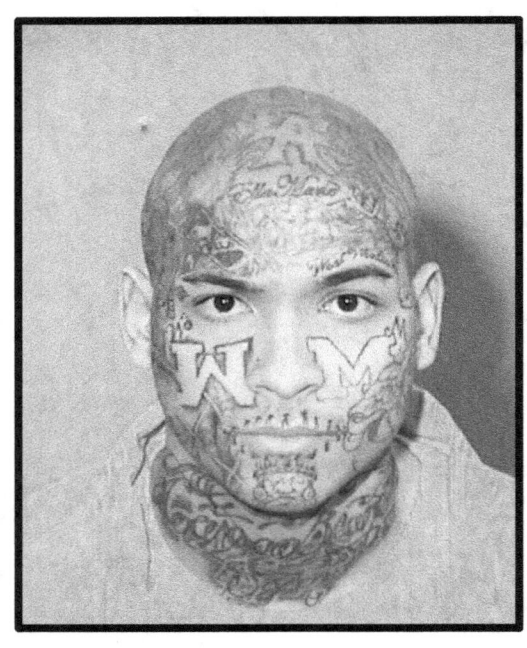

DISTINGUISHING TATS: "W" & "M" ON LEFT AND RIGHT CHEEKSTO REFER TO "WEST MAFIA," STITCHED LIPS, ACE OF SPADES CARD ON RIGHT TEMPLE, AZTEC HEAD ON CHIN, 3 DOTS NEAR LEFT EYE SIGNIFY "MI VIDA LOCA"

DOB: 4/21/1994
ARREST DATES: 10/19/2015, 1/03/2016
CHARGES: DRUG PARAPHERNALIA-POSSESS/USE, THEFT-CONTROL PROPERTY, BURGLARY 2ND DEGREE
RANGE: CALIFORNIA, ARIZONA, COLORADO
GANG AFFILIATION: UNCLEAR

NOTES: UNCLEAR IF "WEST MAFIA" IS PART OF MEXICAN MAFIA PRISON GANG OR A SMALLER GANG LOCAL TO PHOENIX

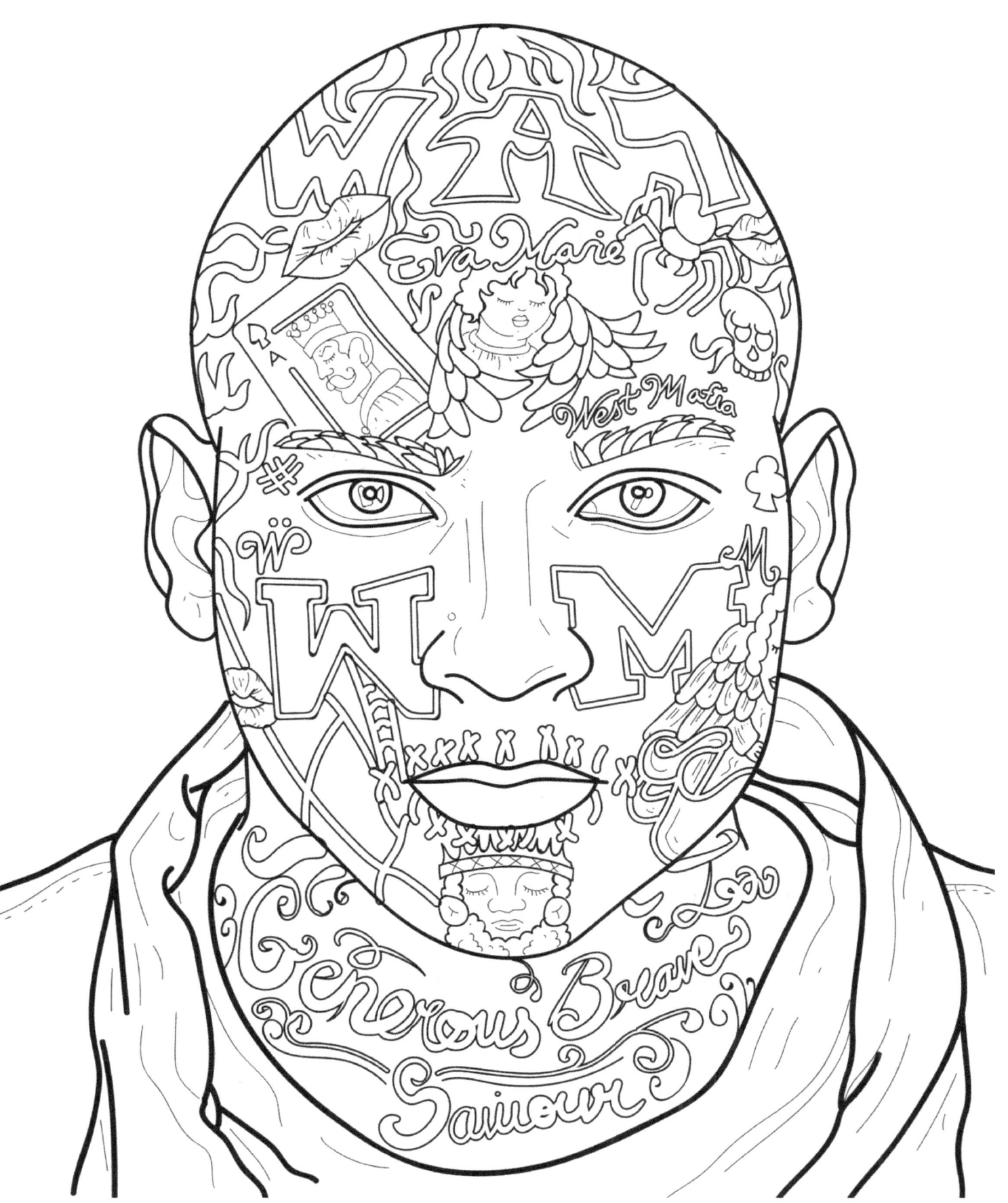

Jerome Smith

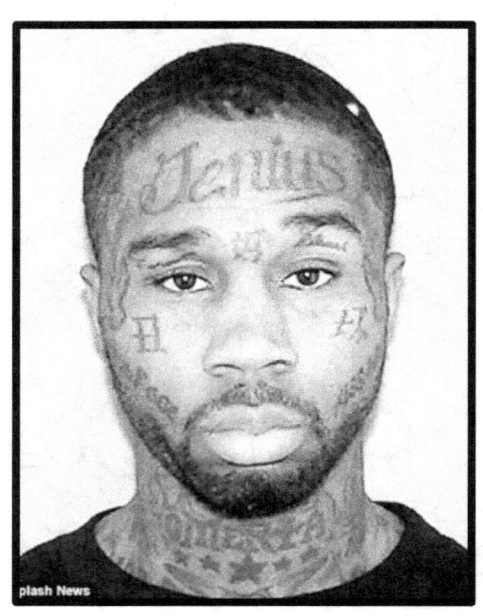

DISTINGUISHING TATS: "GENIUS" ON FOREHEAD, "OMERTA" ON NECK.

DOB: 11/28/1983,
ARREST DATES: 2/01/2011, 5/10/2015,
CHARGES: AGG ROBBERY-ARMED F1, HAVE WEAPN-DRUG RELATED CONVF4, POSS ILLEG DRUG PARAPHENALIA, OBSTRUCT OFFICIAL BUSINESS M2, IMPROPER LIGHTS, TINTED WINDOW VIOLATION, DRIVING WITHOUT LICENSE, FELONIOUS ASSAULT F2
RANGE: HAMILTON COUNTY OHIO
GANG AFFILIATION: UNKNOWN

NOTES: ACCUSED OF STRIKING AN EIGHT-MONTH PREGNANT WOMAN IN THE HEAD WITH A GUN, SAID AN AFFIDAVIT FILED IN HAMILTON COUNTY MUNICIPAL COURT, CINCINNATI, OHIO.

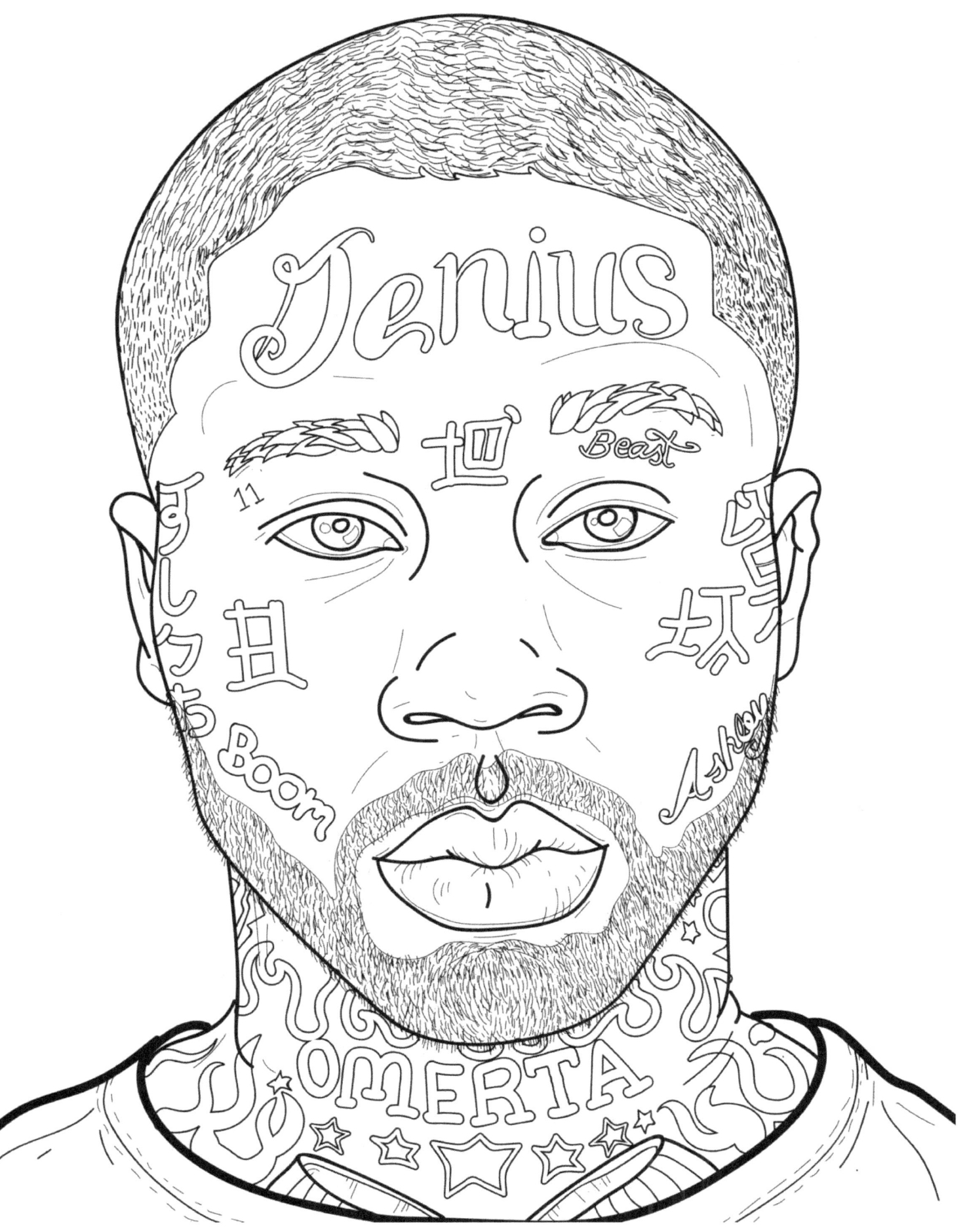

Jason Barnum AKA "Eyeball"

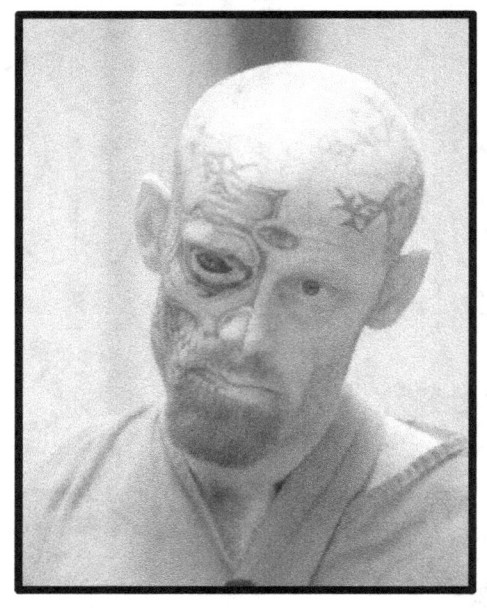

DISTINGUISHING TATS: 3RD EYE ON FOREHEAD, CROWN OF THORNS, SKULL ON TOP OF HEAD, SKELETON SKULL TEETH ON RIGHT SIDE OF MOUTH, RIGHT EYEBALL TATTOOED BLACK

DOB: 4/29/1975
ARREST DATES: 5/01/2010,
CHARGES: CONTROLLED SUBSTANCES IN SCHEDULE I-I(FOR RESALE)(COCAINE), DRIVING ON REVOKED/SUSPENDED LICENSE, ATTEMPTED MURDER 1ST
RANGE: RHEA COUNTY, TN TO ANCHORAGE BOROUGH, AK.
GANG AFFILIATION: UNKNOWN

NOTES: HEROIN ADDICT FUELED ADDICTION BY BURGLARIZING HOMES. SENTENCED TO 22 YEARS IN PRISON FOR SHOOTING ANCHORAGE POLICE OFFICER

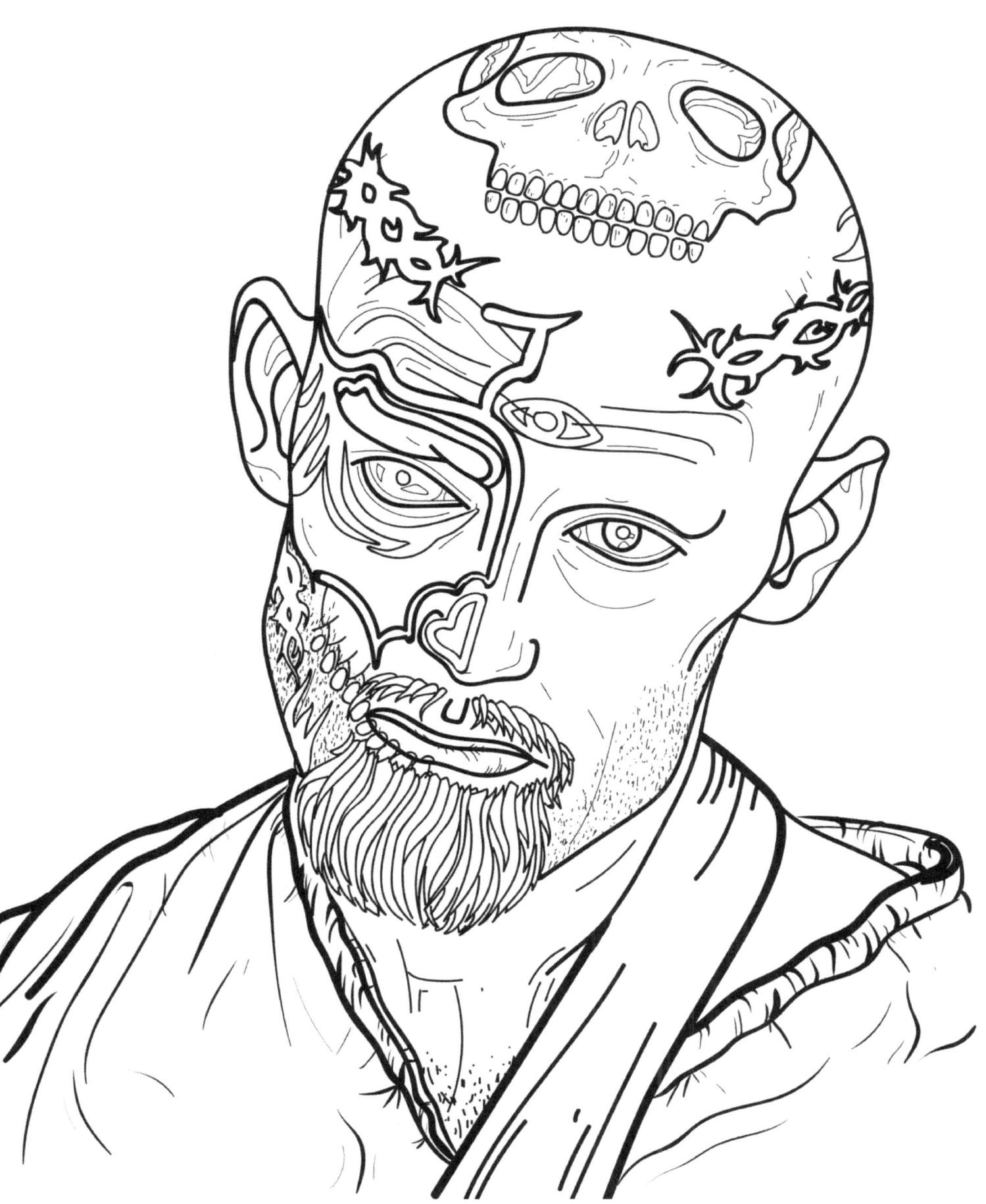

Antoine Petty

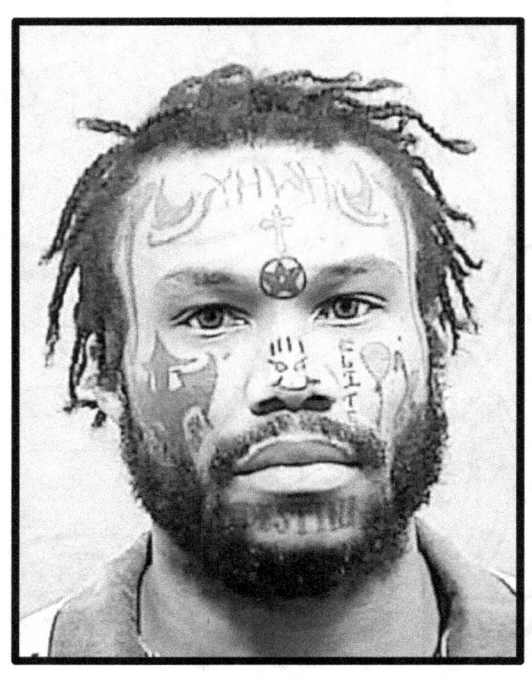

DISTINGUISHING TATS: SMILEY FACE ON NOSE, DEVIL HORNS ON FOREHEAD, "DISTINI" ON CHIN, BALLOON ON LEFT CHEEK

DOB: UNKNOWN
ARREST DATES: 2002, 2014, 2016
CHARGES: THEFT, ASSAULT, MURDER
RANGE: PRINCE GEORGE'S COUNTY MARYLAND. PETTY WAS KNOWN TO FREQUENT THE LARGO AND FORESTVILLE AREAS.
GANG AFFILIATION: UNKNOWN

NOTES: GUILTY OF PUNCHING HIS BABY IN THE FACE UNTIL THE INFANT DIED. SENTENCED TO 40 YEARS IN PRISON.

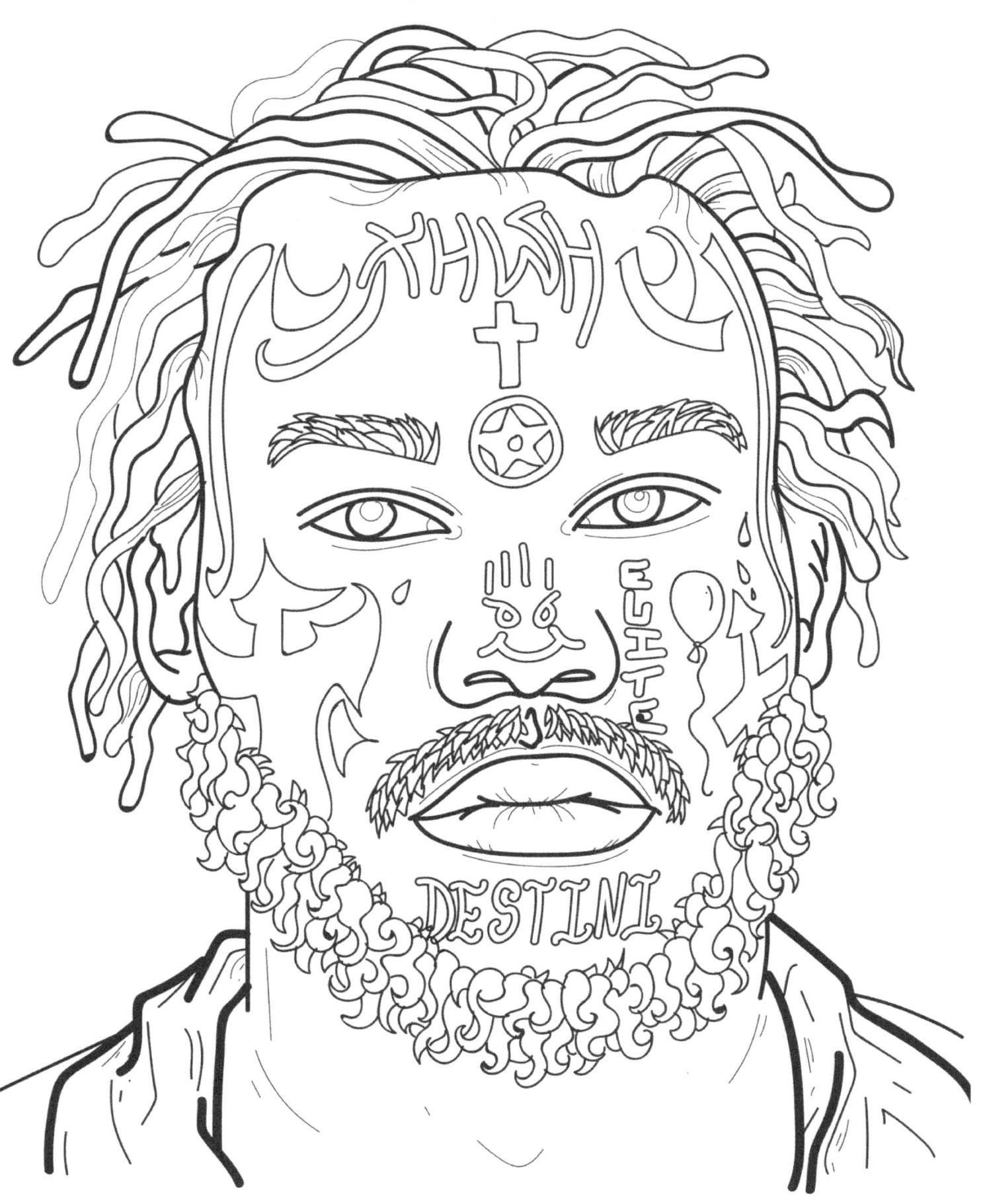

Attributions

Maori Chief.
Published 1784; probably sketched in 1769
Parkinson, Sydney, 1745-1771. Parkinson was the artist on Captain Cook's 1st voyage to New Zealand in 1769. From: Parkinson, Sydney. A journal of a voyage to the South Seas. London, 1784, plate 16, opposite page 90. - Alexander Turnbull Library Reference: PUBL-0037-16. Image is in Public Domain.

Color Test Page
Uzi gun icon designed by Nikita Golubev from www.flaticon.com

Grenade icon designed by Nikita Golubev from www.flaticon.com

Tear drop icon designed by Good Ware from www.flaticon.com

Spider Web icon designed by Freepik from www.flaticon.com

La Catrina icon designed by Freepik from www.flaticon.com

Dollar sign icon designed by Freepik from www.flaticon.com

Star icon designed by Freepik from www.flaticon.com

Mug Shot Face Tattoo Illustrations
The following freelance illustrator worked her face off drawing these:
Lara Mesanza Burke
https://www.freelancer.com/u/laramesanza
www.laramesanzaburke.com

www.ingramcontent.com/pod-product-compliance
Lightning Source LLC
Chambersburg PA
CBHW081649220526

45468CB00009B/2593